This book is dedicated to all those people who keep 'em flying.

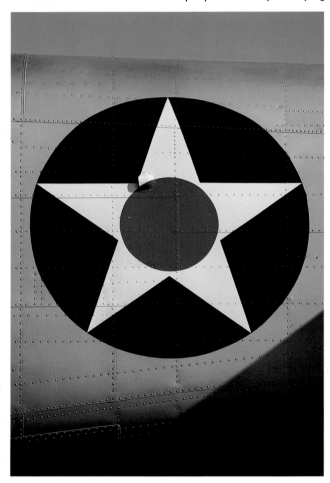

Designed by Marilyn F. Appleby
Edited by Ross A. Howell, Jr., and Kathleen D. Valenzi,
with the assistance of Karen M. Cauthen, Carlotta M. Eike,
Joan Berry Horen, and Gina M. Wallace.
Photography copyright © 1987 by Mark Meyer. All rights reserved.
Introduction copyright © 1987 by Walter J. Boyne. All rights reserved.
This book, or any portions thereof, may not be reproduced
or transmitted in any form or by any means, electronic or mechanical,
including photocopying, recording, or by any information storage and
retrieval system, without permission in writing from the publisher.
Photography may not be reproduced without permission of Mark Meyer.
The introduction may not be reproduced without permission of Walter J. Boyne.
Library of Congress Catalog Card Number 87-80777
ISBN 0-9616878-6-X
Printed and bound in Japan by Dai Nippon Printing Co., Ltd.
Published by Howell Press, Inc., 2000 Holiday Drive,
Charlottesville, Virginia 22901. Telephone (804) 977-4006.
First edition

HOWELL PRESS

CLASSICS

U.S. AIRCRAFT OF WORLD WAR II

PHOTOGRAPHY BY MARK MEYER

INTRODUCTION BY WALTER J. BOYNE

Is there a rational explanation for grown men and women spending thousands of dollars and the best years of their lives coaxing 40-year-old airplanes back into the air? If you are romantic, if your heart beats faster when *The Star Spangled Banner* is played, if you like old movies and old cars, then you know that there are many explanations. It would be flip, however, to dismiss the booming interest in classics as mere patriotism and nostalgia when there are far more meaningful psychological, aesthetic, and engineering reasons. These glamorous veterans tell us much about ourselves as they slip through the sky in evocation of the past.

Yet patriotism and nostalgia are certainly important. Some wars just seem better than others. None are good while they are in progress, but after the passage of time, the public begins to take a fancy to certain of them. The Revolutionary War and the War of 1812 never seemed to take hold, nor did the Mexican or Spanish-American wars. The Civil War, the most terrible conflict experienced by the United States in terms of casualties, gained an almost immediate affection, so much so that the names of Confederate generals soon graced military posts of the very nation they had fought against. The first World War was simply too horrible to capture people's imaginations, although the flyers of that war have been glamorized to some degree. The Korean War has been forgotten, and we are just witnessing the beginning of popular interest in the terrible experience of Viet Nam.

But, ah,…World War II, a vintage war with memories for everyone. Americans shared an absolute gut-feeling that it was a good war, that we were the good guys. Our enemies were demonstrably, irrevocably evil, and their defeat was sure to be welcomed, even by their own people.

It was not only that we were fighting for the right cause; the war changed the country, pulling it laughing and proud from the depths of a major depression. It showed us strengths we didn't know that we had, developing the economy so that our influence extended throughout the world. And the most obvious symbols of this enormous change were our Army, Navy, and Marine air forces. Who would forget that airpower bombed us into the war on December 7, 1941, or that it bombed our way out in 1945?

Our engineering achievements were phenomenal. In 1939 aviation was a cottage industry in the United States, building a few thousand relatively simple airplanes annually. By 1941 we had enough warning to develop a wider base, but we were still naive when it came to war-making, producing airplanes with armor, armament, and equipment not greatly different from those used in 1918. Production levels seemed impossibly high compared to the past, but it was just the beginning. Not only would vastly more aircraft be produced (300,000 airplanes delivered—at a cost of $45 billion), but they were far more complex. The war had begun with the bombing of Pearl Harbor and with lovely, but impotent, Martin B-10s and Boeing P-26s being blown to pieces at Clark Field. It ended less than four years later with Boeing B-29 Superfortress bombers and North American P-51 Mustang fighters ranging over the heart of Japan, unable to find targets worth destroying.

Certainly, the major reason for the resurgent interest in classics is their sheer aesthetic appeal. These lovely fighter and bomber aircraft, from Hellcat to Marauder, from Jug to Liberator, from Corsair to Texan, have a unique quality not found elsewhere in the world of art. Absolutely beautiful sculptures at rest, they transform themselves into transcendental, kinetic masterpieces in flight. This is the change which stirs our souls, and this is what Mark Meyer has captured on film. The alteration is elusive; thousands of photographs of aircraft are just that—pictures of planes. To capture the inner beauty, the photographer must be in resonance with the subject in order to frame with his lens the airframe's latent beauty.

The transformation Meyer seeks begins with soft buzzes and clicks as electrical power is connected. It builds with a mechanical banging as control surfaces are checked, hatches are opened and closed, and commands are shouted from pilot to ground. The whining starter is drowned out by the rise and fall of random explosions merging into coughs of blue-white smoke as the engine rumbles to life. Shouted commands can no longer be heard—hand signals cause the chocks to be pulled, and the airplane lurches forward, still not fully formed, still ground-bound. Not until after the takeoff, when the gear and flaps are up, when the power roars, not to overcome the friction of earth but to summon flight from the sky, is the change complete.

And it is in the air that art and metal truly merge. On the ground the aerodynamic forces tug in one direction only—to the ground. In flight there are infinite vectors of direction. Lift sucks upward, not only at the cambered wings, but on the fuselage as well. It pulls both up and down on the tail, giving variations on its own theme. The airplane seems to duck to shed drag, to rid itself of the encumbrances to flight. The thrust pours back from the engine and propellers, swirling streamlines of moisture to mix with thin trails of exhaust smoke.

And there is still, and always, gravity, overcome in level flight by the other members of the famous lift/drag/thrust/weight equation, but reimposed in doubled or tripled terms with every steep turn. The induced "gravitational" change, known as g force, is evident on a human body inside the aircraft; outside, its subtle evidence can be fixed only by a photographer in tune with his subject, who can collect on film the invisible forces that raise airframe to artwork.

It's a miracle that any are left to see. America proved that it could demobilize even faster than it mobilized, and thousands of aircraft were disposed of brutally. Some spent months or years baking in the desert sun before being cut up to become pots and pans; others were simply crumpled by bulldozers and dumped into land fill. It was not only the return to peace that caused the wastage; the debut of the jet engine seemed to render any World War II airplane obsolete.

Yet some lingered on. The Learjet and its brethren were still in the future, so many companies converted Douglas Invaders, Martin Marauders, and North American Mitchells purchased from war surplus stocks at bargain-basement prices into executive planes. They were expensive to operate, but they were the fastest things around, and for many they exemplified a time that would never come again. The racing community naturally embraced the fighters, never dreaming that the hot new unlimiteds of 1947 would be the hot old unlimiteds of 1987. Many of the famous transport warbirds—C-46s, C-47s, C-54s—went either to civil work or to smaller wars. And then there were the sentimentalists, people who just liked the airplane they flew—or didn't get to fly—and who couldn't resist buying their love object at giveaway prices.

Thus it is that we can enjoy whole formations of immaculate Mustangs more than four decades after test pilot Vance Breese took the first North American NA-73X from Mines Field in 1940. Other types are in shorter supply. There are only a handful of Wildcat, Hellcat, and Thunderbolt fighters still flying. As the cost of operation goes up, the number of aircraft operating goes down. Only one B-29 Superfortress bomber, the fabulous Fifi, stays in the air. A Martin Marauder bomber, lovingly restored by the Confederate Air Force, was airborne for a while, and will be again. There are enough B-25 Mitchell bombers and two-engined Catalinas, flying boats once used for bombing and rescue, to last us, and a comparative surplus of Gooney Bird transports.

Perhaps the only thing of which you can be sure, however, is that you can't be sure of anything. Twenty years ago, no one would have believed that restorers could reach deep into the New Guinea jungles and bring forth Japanese fighters to fly again. Who would have thought that four Halberstadt ground-attack planes from World War I would survive in the attic of a German town hall until the 1970s, complete with spare engines, fitted and lined tool kits, yards of camouflage fabric, handbooks—the time capsule of a squadron repair shop? And then there are the grandiose projects, like the rescue of four Lockheed P-38 Lightnings and the odd B-17 Flying Fortress immured in 40 feet of snow in Greenland for four decades. Never say never. There were no German Daimler-Benz-engined Messerschmitt Bf 109 fighters flying anywhere in the years after the war, nor any French Dewoitine D 520 fighters. Suddenly, one of each was flying in its native country. Sadly, just as suddenly, both were totally destroyed in accidents. Of this, more later.

Undoubtedly part of the lure of these machines is the satisfaction of transforming a battered and rusted hulk into an accurately, painstakingly restored showpiece. The restorer experiences a sense of fulfillment at locating a neglected warbird and cleverly procuring it at the lowest possible price (possibly for only a mortgage on your house). There are some difficulties on the way, beginning with the back-breaking labor of hauling it from its resting place on a flatbed truck to a hangar whose rent seems to go up monthly. It is in this process that one finds that a disassembled aircraft handles nothing like an assembled one; there are no pick-up points to facilitate any necessary rigging, no known centers of gravity to help determine points of balance. A fighter fuselage with engine installed is a wild and fractious thing, with a headstrong center of gravity so far forward that it sheds ropes and tag lines and threatens to tip forklifts over. These are the troubles that are considered fun in retrospect, made easier by the knowledge that you have a nascent classic. The picture of the future, when the tired shards are transformed into something spectacular, is

enough to keep you going. If it doesn't have an engine, or tires, or landing gear, there is always Trade-A-Plane, and it's only money.

Oddly enough, engines and tires and landing gears will not be the major problem. The real difficulties come in getting the hydraulic accumulators, the bomb racks, the thousand other bits that make up the equipment list. The time-consuming and arduous process is punctuated by sudden finds and by abject disappointments. The long-sought generator, supposedly unavailable anywhere, materializes at an airport a mere 800 miles away. After a quick flight over and the money changes hands (it's *only* money, remember), you find that it won't fit because your warbird was modified. But there are other kinds of luck as well; nowhere in the world is the radiator you need—except by chance in the garage down the street, in the box, mint, and cheap.

It is a process familiar to automobile collectors, but much more rarified. For as the hulk slowly changes, as the rust disappears and the parts come together, the restorer becomes ever more conscious that this bird is going to fly, and that the parts can't just look right—they have to *be* right.

Restoration calls for all the elements of backyard, shade-tree, mechanical genius to be combined with the evaluative eye of a surgeon. Can a piston be swapped from one engine to another? How much of the metal will have to be replaced when the reskinning starts? Will you be able to use synthetic materials in the seals? These questions take on added significance when you consider the amount of careful scrutiny your aircraft will undergo once restoration is complete. When you are finished, the layman will admire the airplane extravagantly, but there are experts lurking out there who will not hesitate to point out that Technical Order 1894478, a military document dated 3 August 1943, moved the fuel stencil eight inches to the left of where you have it. If you have to strip the paint and repaint it to move the stencil, well, that's the price of perfection. In this case, money isn't the issue—it's a matter of honor.

Even though it seems a distant thing for most of the restoration, the question of flying the aircraft is always uppermost in your mind. Why worry about flying when you cannot find an intake manifold, a control run, or a starter motor? But as each of these is located, the thrill is allayed by the nagging realization that you are one step closer to first flight day.

There are a number of attitudes that can be adopted at this point, ranging from the stupid to the cowardly, and cowardly is best. On the one hand, you can reason, "Well, I've got two hundred hours in a Comanche, so I'll take six hours in the back seat of a T-6 trainer and then test this single-engine Corsair fighter myself. I just won't make any sudden power applications." Or you can say, "I'll find a pilot current in the airplane, offer him a fee to test-fly this bent-wing dude for me, pay his expenses,..." and live a lot longer.

It doesn't have to be a fighter plane to bite you, either. Even a newly restored T-6 can be a handful to a Piper Cub pilot, and any multi-engine airplane has the strong possibility of engine-out operation.

The passage of 40 years has not made the elegant classic aircraft any less an example of engineering prowess. These warbirds were not designed as toys for weekend flying, but rather as killing machines, or as machines to train people for killing machines. For many restorers, being familiar with a particular line of aircraft and establishing a close, hands-on relationship during the process of rebuilding tends to mask the truth of the plane's sophistication. The argument "I'll be flying it light" is often made as a reason to discount the demanding characteristics of a warplane. This argument is true in part. A P-47 "Jug" Thunderbolt at a maximum gross weight of 15,000 pounds, laden with eight machine guns, 3,400 rounds of ammunition, a 200-gallon external tank, rockets and bombs, and operating from a grass field is far different from your stripped-down Jug weighing in at 11,000 pounds lifting off from a concrete airstrip. The lighter weight is offset by quicker acceleration, which means that the powerful torque will get at you that much sooner. Plus you have 40-year-old systems—oil coolers, intercoolers, whatever—all of which can get you into deep trouble.

The question of pilot proficiency is double-edged, as well, for a great deal of flight time can be as hazardous as too little. To use a pop-psychology cliche—what one needs is "quality time." During the war, young pilots were brought along in hectic procession on trainers like the PT-17s, BT-13s, and AT-6s. From there they may have moved on to the P-40 Warhawk single-engine fighter before receiving instruction on other types of almost new airplanes. Their flying experience was intense, recent, and closely supervised. Even today's 50-year-old airline pilot, veteran of 25,000 hours (22,000 on the autopilot) does not have the level of consciousness needed to handle a hot, 40-year-old fighter.

The previously mentioned Messerschmitt and Dewoitine crashes are perfect examples. Both aircraft were carefully and professionally restored with no expense spared and with the resources of their respective national air forces behind them. Both were flown by highly experienced jet test pilots. In the case of the Messerschmitt, it was destroyed in an accident representative of the kind that occurred so often during the war. The pilot lost control on takeoff, and the beautifully restored "Gustav," its Daimler-Benz engine sonorously pouring forth power, impacted in a parking lot full of cars. As for the test pilot of the Dewoitine D 520, he was well aware of the hot little fighter's tendency to flick-roll if too much back pressure was applied, because veterans had told him that at certain airspeeds and g forces, just a hint of pressure on the stick could send it rolling. He was only unaware of how *little* pressure and how *fast* the roll, and in this case, the airplane flick-rolled him into the ground.

The primary cause of both accidents was the pilot's

lack of experience in handling one of the airplane's peculiarities, the result of inevitable compromises by which the designers achieved performance at the cost of docile handling. Nothing in the training of the two test pilots, even their awareness of the hazards, could have prepared them to react in time to avoid an accident. So what chance does the pilot of a small, private plane like the Bonanza have?

Well, pretty good—if he is extraordinarily careful at all times, if he trains himself carefully, and if his maintenance practices are superb. After learning the hard way, the Confederate Air Force, which has done so much to keep the classic airplanes flying, developed a rigorous program to make the flying safe. There is certainly no easy way, no offhand way, and no inexpensive way to learn to fly these aircraft properly.

This isn't fate, or bureaucracy, or anything else we normally blame things on. It is the direct result of the very thing that contributed to the beauty of the classics—their strong engineering heritage. When you look at a B-17, you are seeing more than crafted metal. The genius of dozens of men and women, poured out over many years in various airplanes and engines, all comes together in this proud Fortress. What you see is the entrepreneurial daring of William Boeing, who stood willing time and again to risk his total assets on the skill of his engineers. It embodies the vision of Claire Egtvedt, who chose to interpret the "multiengine" Army specification as meaning four engines instead of the two the Air Corps had in mind. Boeing engineers had already labored over the Monomail and B-9 prototypes, and had won no contracts. They had fashioned the revolutionary 247 transport, only to see Douglas sweep the board with its DC series. Think of the courage required of management to persist in building big, multi-engine bombers when Boeing was already well established in the fighter field with the P-26. Stockholders were as demanding then as now, so it took incredible courage for 24-year-old Ed

Wells to undertake as assistant project engineer, the supersecret Model 299 which became the Fortress.

The engines which powered the Fortress—Pratt & Whitney R-1690Es on the prototype and Wright R-1820s on the production aircraft—were themselves the result of industrial daring, genius, and years of sweat. Charles Lawrance, creator of the basic layout for the modern radial engine, had started the process. Frederick B. Rentschler brought it along, first at Wright, then later at Pratt & Whitney, where he created a new line of air-cooled radial engines. Both Lawrance and Rentschler were backed by foresighted military men who took chances with their careers and with government money to support their efforts—like Commander Jerome C. Hunsaker, who gambled on Lawrance, and Rear Admiral William A. Moffett, who supported both Wright and Pratt & Whitney at considerable risk.

The superchargers that Dr. Sanford Moss, a grey-bearded patrician, began working on for General Electric in 1918 were a similar product of toil, brains, and love. Altitude records were being set with the supercharger, a device that forced air into the combustion process of an airplane, by the early 1920s, but it took years of experimentation and improvement in the metals used on turbine wheels before the supercharger was capable of the wide use it received in WWII. Neither the B-24 nor the B-17 bombers could have made it over Germany at safe, high altitudes without it. In the process of its development, forgotten men like George A. Hallet, Opie Chenoweth, Ernest T. Jones, and C. Fayette Taylor contributed their invaluable knowledge and expertise to the project.

Thunderbolt, the rugged Republic P-47 single-engine fighter, has a similar heroic ancestry, this time stemming in large part from immigrant Russians. Alexander P. de Seversky, whose father had been the first man to own and fly an airplane in Russia, was infused with a love of flying himself, so he entered the Imperial Russian Naval Air Ser vice in 1914. Shot down and severely injured, de Seversky lost his right leg as a result of the accident. But this did not diminish his love for flight; in fact, it barely slowed him down, because as soon as he was able, he returned to combat and became a 13-victory ace. Sent to the United States by his government, de Seversky elected to stay when he learned that the Bolsheviks had taken over his homeland. While in the States, this inventive genius sold 364 patents to the U.S. government and established his own firm, the Seversky Aircraft Corporation. One of his first products— aircraft skis with an innovative shock-absorber system that he would use again later to good advantage—seemed a natural one for a Russian inventor.

Another Russian, Alexander Kartveli, fled the Russian revolution by going to France, where in 1927 he met the flamboyant Charles Levine. Levine, Clarence Chamberlin's backer and "co-pilot" on the famous flight of the Bellanca "Columbia," established a small aircraft manufacturing business where Kartveli designed two airplane prototypes, the "Uncle Sam" and the "Triad." Neither was successful, largely because of Levine's interference. When de Seversky opened the Seversky Aircraft Corporation, he hired fellow countryman Kartveli away from Levine and made him assistant chief engineer. Ironically, the Russian revolution was a great boon to U.S. aviation, sending us Igor Sikorsky and vast numbers of skilled craftsmen, as well as de Seversky and Kartveli.

Kartveli's first design for Seversky, the SEV-3, was a three-seat floatplane that set records and clearly forecast the form the Thunderbolt would take. It was radial-engined, all metal, with a round fuselage and elegant, elliptical wings. The Kartveli touch which would become so famous— smoothly rounded surfaces, generous fillets, the appearance of raw power—was evident in the SEV-3.

Seversky and Kartveli both believed in intensive development of their basic airplane, and there followed a suc-

cession of evolutionary designs which led from the BT-8 trainer, notorious for ground looping, through the P-35, which won an order for 77 aircraft in 1936 and which was the predecessor of the P-47.

Major de Seversky was a talented engineer, pilot, and showman, but he was not the best businessman in the world, and Seversky Aircraft Corporation had to be reorganized as the Republic Aircraft Corporation. De Seversky was out, but Kartveli remained and extended his formula through XP-41 and XP-43 variations, prototypes to the P-47. At the time he was almost alone in America in selecting radial engines for Army Air Force fighters.

The big breakthrough for Kartveli came with the introduction of the enormous Pratt & Whitney R-2800 engine. It was the perfect marriage of airframe and engine heritage, the latter carrying with it the contributions of Sanford Moss. The P-47 emerged as the biggest single-place fighter ever built—a brawling bruiser capable of taking enormous punishment and coming back home. Given that 15,683 were built, it is tragic that so few survive today.

The P-47's younger and generally more popular rival, the North American P-51 Mustang, was produced by a "new" company with an even richer development history. There was a heavy Teutonic influence on the P-51, and not because the head of the company, West Virginian James Howard Kindelberger, was known as "Dutch." The Teutonic influence comes, in part, from one of the principal contributors to the P-51's design, German-born Edgar Schmued. Don Berlin, father of both the P-40 fighter and the XP-46 prototype, was also an important factor. But there probably wouldn't have been any aircraft from the firm if it hadn't been for a real Dutchman, Tony Fokker. Fokker founded the Atlantic Aircraft Corporation in May 1924, and the company became, over time and via a convoluted family tree, North American Aviation. This family tree included Curtiss Aeroplane and Motor Company, Douglas Aircraft,

General Motors, American Dornier, Berliner/Joyce, Sherman Fairchild's American Aviation Corporation, and the automobile flavor of the Cord Corporation, all melding somehow down into the General Aviation Corporation, which was converted to the immensely successful North American Aviation under Kindelberger.

The P-51's gene pool is further enriched by its engine, starting with the American Allison, then switching to the Rolls-Royce Merlin, whose own existence can be traced back to the inspiration—or at least the instigation—of the Curtiss V-12! Thus the lovely P-51 Mustangs are the refined product of a rich admixture of almost all of American aviation, and a good bit of German and British as well.

This same vital historic process can be found to greater or lesser degrees in any of the warbirds. The mixed heritage of genius is undoubtedly responsible for the high degree of performance of which the airplanes were capable. This in turn has inspired the legends about them.

Perhaps the best measure of the high level of performance they achieved is found in the unlimited racers, those airplanes that can be improved upon without restriction. Some of the same airframes built in 1944 or 1945 and which began their racing careers in 1946 are still racing today. They are more and more modified, and some of the artisans of refinement talk about the piston-engine Mustang attaining speeds of 600 miles per hour! One can imagine Edgar Schmued looking down with benevolent pride when that happens.

But there are other roads to fame. Boeing B-17s were modified for fire-bombing and served valiantly for years in the toughest of conditions before undergoing restorations. Beech C-45s, after returning to executive service, took on yet another demanding career in flying cargo—chiefly bank checks—at night, in all weather, in all seasons. Transport aircraft drifted into U.S. feeder lines, then migrated to South American lines, often returning many years later on a one-way trip to an abandoned airstrip carrying the stuff that makes funny cigarettes. And then there are the incredibly resilient T-28 and T-34 trainers that spent years being bounced into the ground by ham-handed student pilots before entering restoration.

Planes have been reclaimed from watery graves, dragged up from years of submersion to be judged worthy of restoration. But there are happier examples too. Some planes were flown for just a few hundred hours and then put into extended storage. When these are discovered, the process of restoration is much easier.

But no matter what the history, no matter what the risk, the real secret of why men and women spend their time and fortunes restoring classic warbirds to flight can only be found in the satisfaction it provides them. To be aware that you have created something of beauty from what was once debris, to know that what you have built is sound and airworthy is a marvelous feeling. To sit at the controls and imagine that you are a famous pilot—Dick Bong, or Don Gentile, or Erich Hartmann—that's worth something, too. But perhaps the best answer can be found in the sparkling eyes of the visitors at Oshkosh, Wisconsin, or at Harlingen, Texas, when they see a warbird for the first time. The tiny, grainy images of airplanes found on T.V. programs like "Twelve O'Clock High" or "Ba Ba Blacksheep" are pale shadows of these big, handsome, capable machines. The veteran planes put flesh to imagination and give depth to history, for they are three-dimensional, filled with sounds, redolent of grease, fuel, and hydraulic fluids. Most vividly of all, they are filled with human spirit.

So in the end, the best analogy to the drive to restore airplanes may be a cocktail. Take one part nostalgia, one part patriotism, two parts craftsmanship, and one part admiration for engineering skills; mix; and garnish with public education and adulation. It's a pretty heady drink, one that will keep the skies filled with classics for years to come.

—WALTER J. BOYNE

I was working in a coal mine and attending the Pittsburgh Institute of Aeronautics on weekends. The day after Japan bombed Pearl Harbor, I happened to be at the institute, and my instructor asked me, "Why don't you join the cadets?"

I said, "I don't have any college."

He told me that if I could pass the equivalent of two years of college, I could get in, so right away, I went to the Pittsburgh Post Office and signed up for pilot training as an Army Air Corps cadet. After two months of pre-flight training at Maxwell Field in Montgomery, Alabama, I received the equivalent of two years of college.

When our training was completed, our group went overseas, but my crew was kept behind. They sent us down to Brooksville, Florida, where we were trained to drop glide bombs. You would drop the bombs 20 miles away from the target, and they were supposed to glide on in. We practiced dropping bombs on an uninhabited island in the Bahamas. The month-long glide bombing training was very hush-hush. One guy happened to sneak off the field, and they busted him from second lieutenant down to private just like that.

The B-17 was very easy to fly, and for combat, it was one of the best planes ever built. You could tear that thing half apart, and it would still fly, still respond. We had one guy at our base who was knocked out of formation and German fighters got on him. He out-dove an Fw 190 down to the deck. He had to be doing over 400 mph to out-dive

a fighter, but it held together. The B-17 was tough. Even though it looked awkward on the ground, it was a thing of beauty in flight.

Our flying gear included silk gloves with wool gloves over top of them, and leather on top of those two. If the guns jammed up on a high-altitude mission, you might take off the leather and possibly the wool, but you didn't dare take off the silk gloves because your fingers would freeze right to the guns. It was 65 below at times. There was no heat in the plane of any kind, not like these modern planes which are pressurized. And even if it had been pressurized, in combat, one hole would take care of that.

My first raid was out over the North Sea en route to Norway to drop bombs on heavy-water plants there. We didn't encounter any enemy fighters ourselves, although we saw fighters attacking the group ahead of us. Coming back, though, we passed through a heavy rainstorm. There was no way to see through the windshield—we were flying blind. The only way to keep from running into each other was to look out of the windows on the side.

My second mission was close to the west coast of France. There was a boat that had come in from Japan that was supposed to have something on it. We went after that ship but never bombed it because it was too cloudy. Coming back, just before we crossed the English Channel, an enemy fighter came out of the sun. He killed one man and injured three others. One fellow had his boots blown right off him. A shell had exploded—it must have been a 20mm—at the hydraulic pumps alongside him. All of that damage was done on just one pass by the fighter.

After we got back, the tail gunner got out, looked at the tail of the plane, and turned as white as a piece of paper. You would swear that there was no way a human could have been in that tail and not been killed. It had holes all through it. The plane was shot up so bad that they rolled it off the end of the runway and junked it.

If we saw a stray plane coming at us when we were flying formation, everyone put their guns on him. The Germans had captured some of our aircraft, and they would fly up into formation, shoot down a plane, and then take off. If one of our fighters ever pointed his nose at us, we would shoot him. It was self-preservation, because you didn't know if there was a jerry in that plane or a U.S. pilot.

If I'd have kept my mouth shut, I may not have been shot down. We were scheduled to fly a mission to a ball-bearing plant. I was always flying "tail-end Charlie," the most dangerous position in formation. You're the last one, so enemy fighters come in on you first. Before this mission started, I went to the commanding officer and complained. "Damn it," I said, "I'm tired of flying tail-end Charlie." He said that he'd take care of it. I was put on the lead man's right wing.

In formation only two planes carried bomb sights— usually the leader and one of the wingmen. We were on our bomb run, and the lead man called out on the radio, "Bomb sight's out. Take over." It was my 17th mission—February 25, 1944.

No sooner had he said that than I saw one, two, three jerries. They had been tuned in to our radio frequency, and they evidently thought I had the bomb sight, because they were zeroing in on me. They hit my plane with about three shells, which blew it out of formation a half a mile. One shell went up through the right wing. It didn't explode, but the gas drained right out, so we lost an engine. The impact knocked the oil pressure out on the number two inboard engine—I had to feather that one—and we lost the

supercharger on the number four engine to a burst underneath it. At that altitude, if you don't have your supercharger, you don't have much power. As a result, we only had one good engine, and we were too far away from our own fighters for protection.

Nine German fighters jumped us. During evasive action, I got down too low and had to land in a big, plowed field. During the landing, I kept hollering over the intercom for the crew to get the ball turret gunner out, which they did. In fact, all ten of us got out all right. No one had a scratch.

Once on the ground, I informed the crew about all the parachutes we had been ducking coming down. A B-24 had been hit, and its crew had bailed out. On our descent, I flew right through them while they were floating through the air, barely missing three of the crewmen.

As we were standing in the field, Germans came in from all directions. They marched us into a town called Landau, where a vehicle picked us up along with what they could find of the B-24 crew. They drove us to one of their prisons. We spent the night there with only a wooden bunk to sleep on and a wooden pillow for a headrest. The next day, they took us to Frankfurt for interrogation, and we stayed there two days. Next, they put us in cattle cars, and shipped us to a town in Germany located right on the Baltic. It was 16 miles from Sweden and freedom, but there was a whole war between us.

At the camp, we weren't physically abused, as far as beatings went, but there was never enough to eat. We found out after the Russians came that the warehouse had been full of Red Cross parcels—spam and chocolate bars and cigarettes—that the Germans had been using for themselves.

Normally, we'd get meat the size of a hamburger for the week. There was a zoo in Berlin, and after the city was bombed, the Germans brought in something we swore was elephant meat, because the bones were so big.

In the morning, they'd boil barley to make cereal. We had two thin slices of bread made out of potato, flour, and sawdust. From time to time, the Germans would bring dehydrated turnips in on a wagon, and we'd be on our hands and knees picking up turnips that had fallen through the cracks in the wagons in order to have something extra to eat. I weighed 195 pounds when I went into the camp, 130 pounds when I came out.

There was some sickness among us, but we had a base doctor in camp. In fact, there was also a catholic priest, so we had medicine, both spiritually and physically.

We wrote letters to the people back home, but they were unsealed and about the size of an envelope, so you couldn't say much. At least our families knew we were alive.

The Germans had a shoemaker shop in prison camp, and they asked for people who could resole shoes to work in it. I'd done a little bit—living through the Depression, you had to—so I volunteered. The Red Cross furnished the leather, and we punched an awl through the leather to make a hole for the wooden nails they sent us. It was better than walking barefoot!

One time I concocted a scheme for prisoners to escape. At a prearranged signal, guys would throw mush balls—we had some athletic equipment—into the area between each guard tower and the high fence where they had barbed wire. This would draw the attention of the guards. Then the guy would say he wanted to get the ball inside the barbed wire fence. These guys would hop over the barbed wire, and naturally, the guards would be watching them getting the ball out while another group of guys would go scurrying over and escape. I think we got three or four out the first night, and three or four out the second night.

One morning after I was there 14 or 15 months, we discovered that the Germans had taken off during the night. They had heard that the Russians were in the area, and they were scared to death of them.

Once the Russians took over the camp, you could leave if you wanted to, but they brought in cows and pigs that they'd taken from local farmers, so many people stayed because of the food. Some guys went into the towns. In fact, the natives invited our boys to stay with them, because if an American boy was in their house, the Russians wouldn't bother them.

We stayed with the Russians three or four weeks. One day, B-17s, one after the other, came in and hauled us out to France. I think they moved the whole camp out in about a day—27,000 people. They put us on a train and took us to Camp Lucky Strike. There, the guys went down and traded packs of cigarettes for white bread. That white bread was like cake to us.

All they fed us at Camp Lucky Strike was creamed food. Our stomachs were not fit to eat anything else like potatoes and steaks—just creamed beef and creamed chicken. We tore the camp apart the three or four weeks we spent there waiting to go home.

Finally, "General Ike," General Eisenhower, came. He landed, stood up on the wing of his airplane, and said, "We're doing everything in our power to get you home as fast as we can, so be patient." And about a week later a brand-new boat came over. We loaded all the guys on it. We were sleeping on the deck and every place else. Halfway back, the steering malfunctioned, and we circled around and around and around in the middle of the ocean for half a day or better. The boat finally arrived in Boston, and from there I went home.

Joseph S. Bochna flew a B-17 Flying Fortress with the 526th Squadron, 379th Bombardment Group (Heavy), 8th Army Air Force. Shot down over Germany on his 17th combat mission, he spent 14 months in a prisoner-of-war camp. He received the Air Medal with two Oak Leaf Clusters.

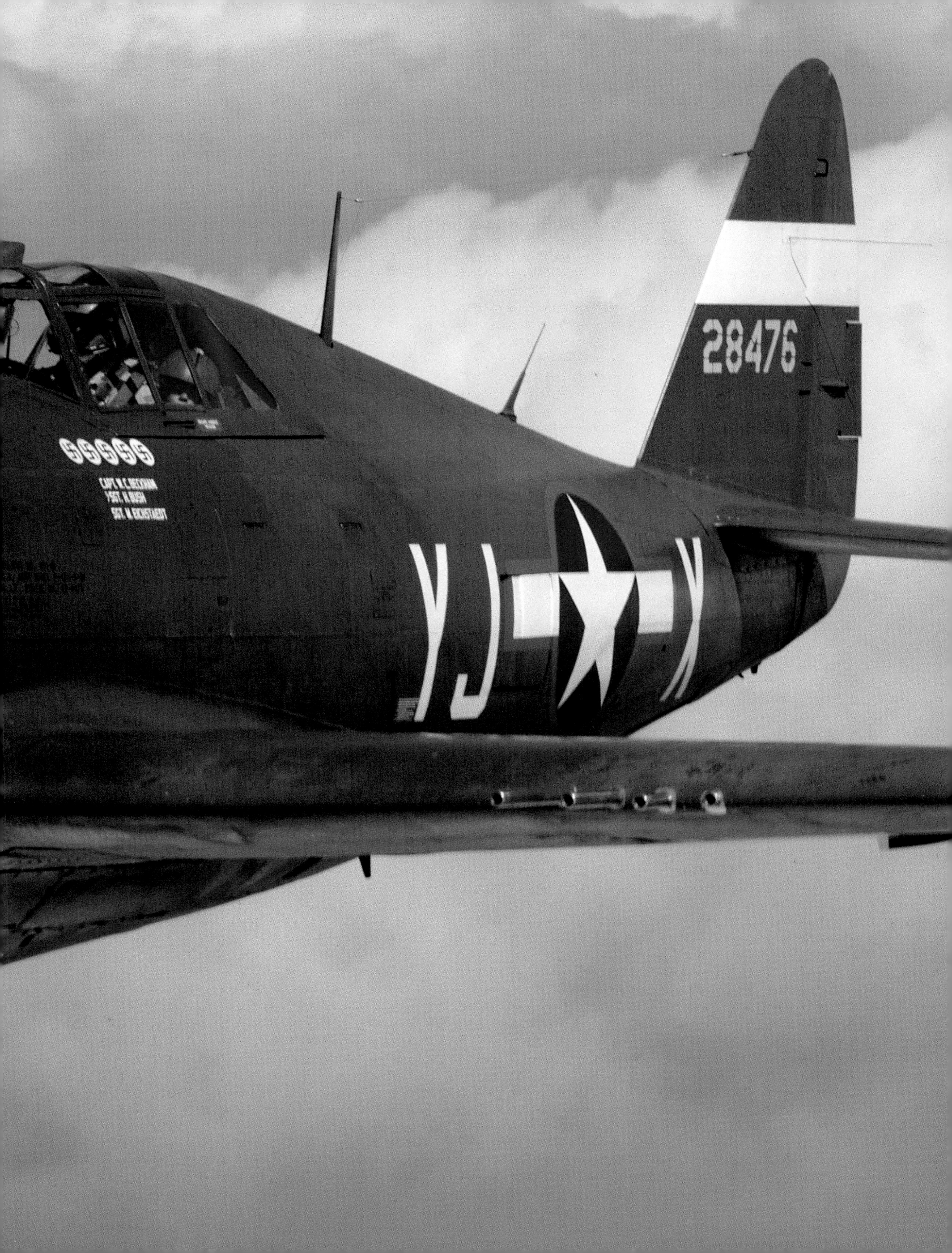
28476
YJ-X

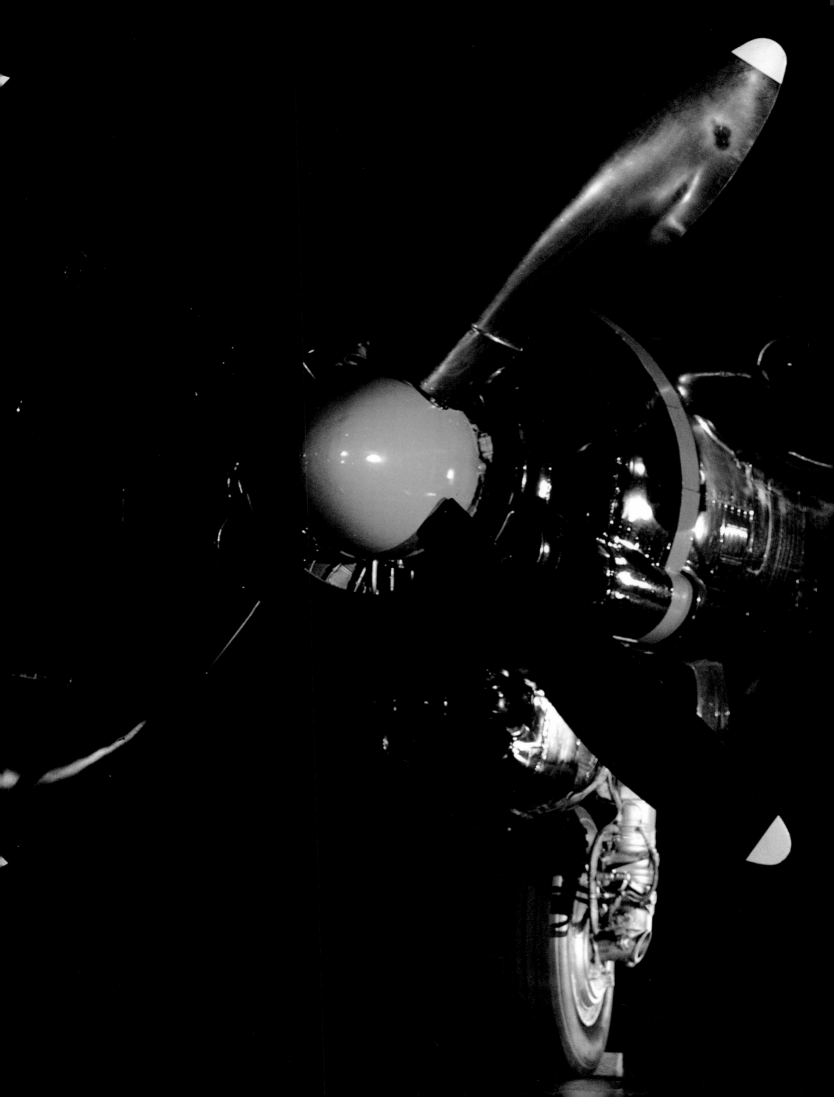

When I graduated from law school in July 1941, I knew I was going into the armed services somewhere, because of selective service. I had come up with a very low draft number, and I decided I'd better make my own choice.

I ended up in the 71st Fighter Squadron, North African Strategic Air Force. There were 13 of us sent over to West Africa on New Year's Eve, 1943, to replace pilots that were lost during the invasion of Africa. I was stationed in Ain-M'Lila, Algeria, which is at the northern head of the Sahara Desert, and I flew 50 missions from there before I came back home in July.

The first mission I remember very well. It was called Biskra, and we were strafing Rommel's troops as they were coming out of Libya. That was in January 1943. We flew north toward Libya along the Mediterranean.

We flew in formation and machine-gunned trucks and tanks and the soldiers that were traveling along with them. Then we got attacked by Me 109s. We lost one fellow, not because he got hit by a fighter, but because he got so low, he flew into a telephone pole.

The Me 109 was a very effective fighter. We ran into a lot of them. I remember one briefing where three of our squadrons were preparing for a mission to bomb a couple of airfields. The intelligence officer who was briefing us said, "In this one field over here there are 142 Me 109s, and in the other field there are 60 more Me 109s," and some jokester in the back of the room said, "And there are 202 of them coming in at 12 o'clock." No matter where we went, it seemed we were outnumbered three-quarters of the time.

When Rommel tried to break through the Kasserine Pass, the Allies had every airplane in North Africa flying through and shooting at whatever was on the ground. Rommel's gunners were up in the hills, shooting down at us, which was a disconcerting experience. That's why I don't fly anymore. I figure I've used up all the luck I ever had.

When Rommel tried to get out of North Africa, the Germans sent everything that could transport anything over to fly out Rommel's troops. We intercepted probably 300 airplanes in the Mediterranean. Everything was there. You'd fly along and see Germans flying past you. Everybody was going everywhere in every direction. I don't think anybody knew what was going on, but we slaughtered them.

I was the lead man on that mission. We were flying on the deck, having been assigned slightly different altitudes. When we found a German aircraft, we shot him. Meanwhile, you kept looking back to make sure they didn't get on your tail. There were so many airplanes there—it was incredible. I imagine we shot down close to 100 aircraft that day.

We didn't make passes, just engaged and kept going. There were too many airplanes around to make passes. I'd see somebody coming in and turn my nose right at him, as did the whole squadron. You'd fire as the enemy was going by, but you didn't see him again, because he'd either be headed somewhere else, or he'd be going down dead. Generally, they don't turn back once they know you've seen them. The best defense a fighter pilot has is to see the other plane before it sees him, or at least before it can get within firing range.

The P-38 was beautiful. Ours carried four 50-caliber

machine guns and one 20mm cannon. Depending on the mission, we'd sometimes carry two 500-pound bombs, or one bomb and one belly tank. If we were going on high-altitude assignments escorting B-17s, we might carry two belly tanks.

The P-38 was unique because it had a steering wheel rather than a stick. Of course, you had control of your ailerons, and when you pushed the column back and forth, it put you up and down.

Firing controls for the machine guns were separate from the cannon. The button for the machine guns was on the top of the steering column, while the cannon controls were on the bottom. You could fire the bullets as tracers out of the machine guns and when you saw they were going in the right direction, you'd use your cannon. I don't think I shot the cannon much at all. I employed it more for ground-support activity since it had greater firepower and would do more damage.

In combat the Lightning had a great advantage in torque. The aircraft had counter-rotating propellers, which meant we could turn very tightly in either direction. Other airplanes could be turned tightly with their torque, but if they were turned against it, they had trouble.

I remember when we left advanced training to go and check out the Lightning, all the boys were telling us that it was dangerous to fly—that you couldn't parachute out.

Inverting the aircraft was one theory for bailing out, but another way was to slow the P-38 down just as slow as you could get it, then get out on the wing, slide on the wing to get down below the boom, and drop. I never wanted to test it, but I knew some fellows who had gotten out that way, so I knew it could be done. The trouble with inverting an airplane and dropping out of it was that there was a good chance that the airplane might continue on its arc, which meant it could end up circling under you as you were parachuting down.

One of the closest calls I had was when we were escorting B-17s in Tunis. There were enemy fighters all over the B-17s, and we were trying to keep them off. The enemy shot down at least one plane and started going after the crewmen who had bailed out. As I pulled out to chase the fighters away from the fellows in parachutes, I looked behind me, and there were two Me 109s back on my left tail, and two more on my right. I was at about 18,000 feet. To avoid them I just went straight down, diving, sweeping the plane back and forth to avoid their fire. I pulled out at about 2,500 feet. When I looked around, there was no one near me.

Unfortunately, by that time I had lost one engine and the whole electrical system of the plane. I had one hole in the canopy, where a bullet had come in behind me and had hit the instrument panel. I flew for a little bit, and then I saw a B-17 heading west. I managed to get my plane up very cautiously underneath the B-17—the gunner saw me coming, but I didn't go rushing in—and I flew underneath that 17 until we were almost to the home base, so that I'd have someone else shooting if there was need for it.

Then I flew over the base, making the normal pattern to land. That's when I found out that my two main wheels wouldn't go down. Only the nose wheel did. I know all the people on the P-38 side of the field saw the trouble I was in, but the bombers used the same field. When I was coming in for final approach, I saw a bomber coming in the other way on the same runway. So I flew my plane down hard into the ground, and that broke the nose wheel, then I bounced back up. I came down, hit the ground, and slid right under the B-17's wing. I didn't fly for two weeks after that incident. It was a hell of a way to land a P-38, but it gave me a lot of confidence in the airplane. I never worried about the Lightning after that.

We got a potful of flying in the invasion of Sicily. We flew two missions a day—once it was three missions in a day. We'd take off at some ungodly hour, go over and do our job, come home, refuel, take off, go back over. During all this time, we'd get out of the plane for 45 minutes, maybe an hour. Missions were constant. Every two or three days, we were totally engaged.

It was a hard life. I was the right age at the time to put up with it. We were on British rations, which meant we got tea with milk in it, mutton about every other meal, and a quart of scotch and gin each month, which only lasted a couple days. Socializing meant either poker or volleyball.

As for gear, sometimes I wore an oxygen mask when flying over 10,000 feet, but we had no anti-g suits. There was weather flying gear, and it was occasionally required, but I preferred not to wear it because it was so bulky. I usually wore just a khaki shirt and trousers, a parachute, a gun, and a canteen. That was it.

I don't ever remember seeing people on the ground. Our primary target on strafing runs was almost always planes on airfields, with the exception of the Kasserine Pass, which was a "must" operation—Rommel was about to break loose and screw up all our plans for trapping him. There I remember strafing troops. Outside of that, our targets were either trucks, airplanes, or tanks. Undoubtedly, people were in them, but you could never allow yourself to think about that. That's one reason I never wanted to be in the infantry. It's possible I killed a number of people. My God, but you had to do it.

I don't think anyone liked strafing. You did it, but you didn't necessarily have to love it. It was one of the worst things you could do, because you knew someone was going to be shooting at you while you were at it.

I remember one time when we were strafing—we were coming back from a bombing mission in Sicily, and there were anti-aircraft guns down below shooting at us. I looked back and saw their tracers going in between the booms of my airplane. I got 72 holes in my Lightning that day.

Once I was a Canadian prisoner. I had gotten separated on a mission coming off a target, and I was flying into the coast of Africa by myself with very little gasoline, when I saw an airstrip. I landed very nicely, happy to have the thing on the ground. Then I raised my canopy, took off my parachute, climbed out on the wing, and a man said, "Put your hands up." Here was this Canadian sergeant with a .45 aimed at me.

I tried to explain to him who I was, but there were other instances of Germans coming into fields. It would take time to confirm my identity, so I spent the night in jail. That evening I had a couple of beers with the Canadians, and we talked. They asked me a lot of questions about the United States, and I'm sure that before the night was over, they were convinced I was a Yank. The next morning they gassed up my plane, and I flew on down to my airfield. That was the only time I was "captured" during the war.

Henry R. Beeson was a P-38 Lightning pilot with the 71st Squadron, 1st Fighter Group, North African Strategic Air Force. He flew 50 combat missions and was awarded the distinguished Flying Cross and the Air Medal with six Oak Leaf Clusters.

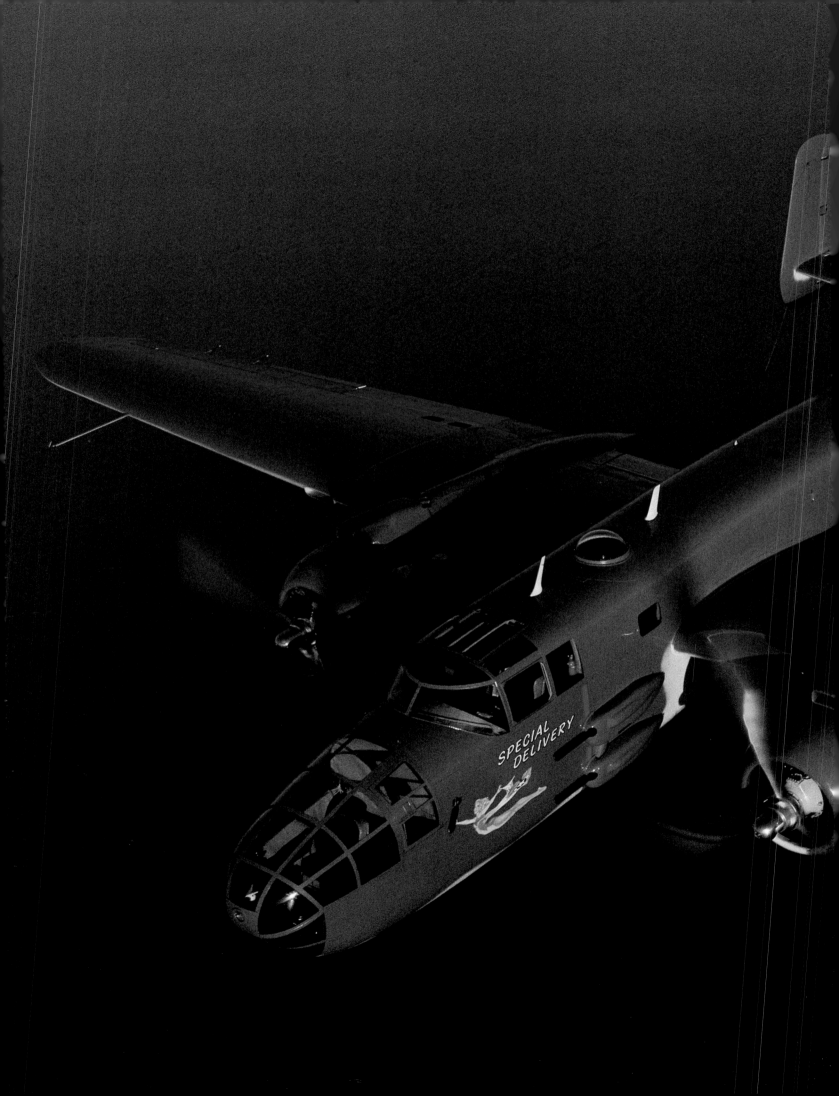

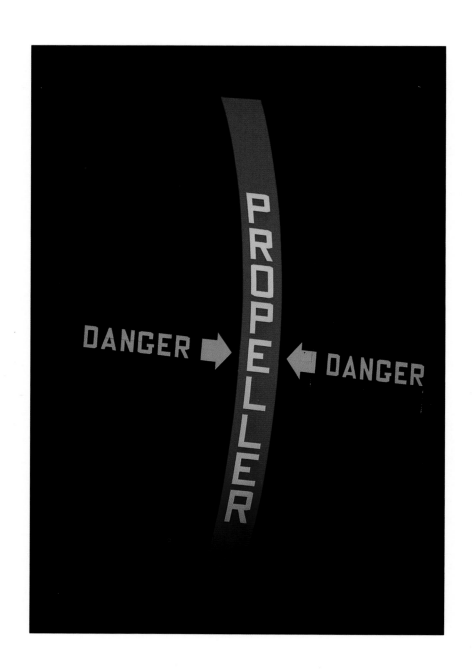

If one thing matches the marvel of the golden age of aviation, it is the legacy left by superb World War II cameramen such as Edward Steichen, Horace Bristol, and Charles Fenno Jacobs. A highly acclaimed photographer, Steichen headed the Navy's special photographic unit during the war and surrounded himself with the best photographers of the time.

These and many other talented photographers not only captured memories from an era but provided documentation of specific events. An unbiased, reliable witness, the camera recorded everything from factory efforts to meet wartime demands for equipment, to aerial strikes by fighters and bombers, to ground combat maneuvers, to naval engagements. From this enormous amount of film, generals and admirals could analyze campaigns for flaws and successes and use the information gathered to plan future military strikes.

WWII photographers directly aided Allied offensive and defensive maneuvers through photoreconnaissance efforts, as well. Aerial photographers recorded enemy emplacements, troop movements, secreted enemy airbases, and hidden fuel depots, using both daylight and infrared films to expose targets to attacks. And when the action in the skies got hot, many aerial photographers set aside their cameras and manned guns, giving them behind-the-scenes experience and a perspective on aerial combat which was reflected in their work. Like the generals who strategized, the crewmen who prepared aircraft and carrier decks, and the pilots who tallied countless successes in the skies, these airborne photographers played a significant role in the Allied victory.

As effective as these skilled photographers were in documentation and photoreconnaissance, they played an even bigger role in maintaining high morale back home. Newspapers and movie-theater newsreels placed images of the Allied war effort before an eager American public, thus sustaining a patriotism that carried the country out of a national Depression and into the war effort wholeheartedly.

Not every wartime photographer was a Steichen, however. Some of the most impressive photographs found in public and private archival collections are the snapshots taken by officers and enlisted men during their tours of duty. Amateur photographers, these men recorded everything about their social and personal lives—camp conditions, company mascots, off-duty recreation, on-duty devotion—reflecting a camaraderie and bonding which still exists today among WWII veterans.

While many years have passed since the end of World War II, the beauty of the photography from that era endures in collections all across the country. Representing one small piece of a large and unique photographic heritage, the *CLASSICS* archival images here, along with news accounts, excerpts from personal diaries, and selections drawn from popular culture, can transport those who lived through the war, as well as those who did not, back to a time when warbirds filled the skies of Europe and the Pacific.

This section is also a reminder that the majestic airplanes of WWII were designed as powerful, lethal warbirds. These airborne weapons caused enormous destruction and resulted in the loss of hundreds of thousands of lives. Brave pilots and crews flew them at great personal risk, and each of them, at one time or another, lost friends, experienced homesickness, and fought off despair, while trying to summon the courage and will to do the job required of them.

Here is a brief memory of that age. It was an age when "classic" aircraft were new and when Americans worked hard to preserve democracy for future generations, at all costs. The memory is bittersweet.

COMBAT CAMERAMEN, TECHNICAL TRAINING SCHOOL

Negotiations with Japan appear to be terminated to all practical purposes with only barest possibilities that Japanese Government might come back and offer to continue. Japanese future action unpredictable but hostile action possible at any moment. If hostilities cannot, repeat cannot, be avoided, the U.S. desires that Japan commit the first overt act.

—message from General George C. Marshall to General Douglas MacArthur, 27 November 1941

HEAVY-BOMBER AIR CREW

**(For physical inspection) we would bend
over in front of one medical officer while
another would look down our throats. If they
didn't see each other, they would hand us a
bible, and we were "in."**

—personal account

P-51 MUSTANG

P-38 LIGHTNINGS

Popular movies included "Thunderbirds," starring Gene Tierny, and "Navy Blues," starring Ann Sheridan. Dancers and romancers enjoyed the popular songs "Begin the Beguine" by Artie Shaw, "Deep Purple" by Tommy Dorsey, and Glenn Miller's "In the Mood."

P-47 THUNDERBOLTS

APRIL 12, 1944. Another big raid—way up into Austria proper. Flew over Austrian Alps, still snow capped, to hit our target, Bad Voslau—an aircraft factory. We were routed to fly right through the flak. We missed the flak, but the ME-110's, JU-88's, ME-109's and FW-190's jumped us right over the target. We got our ship shot up pretty badly. This was the first mission for our new tail gunner and he got hit in the shoulder by a piece of 20mm shell. He had not fired a round yet—only test fired. Most of the tail end of our ship was shot up—but it got us home. I got two big holes (6 to 8 inches each) in my top turret and got a hole in Peyton's (pilot) window. Really, there were holes all over the whole ship. I shot almost all my ammo—everyone did. One JU-88 followed us almost all the way back and kept making passes at us. We saw a B-24 go down and 9 or 10 chutes opened from it. Our engines really caught hell—#1 is the only one that survived the trip…#2 got hit, supercharger shot out and wing hit bad…Lost #3—some mechanical difficulty, of all things…#4 got the carburetor lines shot off of it. We also got some big ones in the wings and another hit on our elevator that screwed up the tabs. I could have stopped the #4 running wild by shutting off the gas line, but we needed its power to bring us home. It was hung at top speed….

We dumped all of our ammo, machine guns and waist guns—and everything we could get loose and that did not pertain to the actual flying of the ship—it went into the Adriatic Sea. If #4 had quit on us, we'd have one and a half engines left and it takes a good healthy two of them to keep that baby in the air. (It took the ground crew a full four weeks to put the plane back together in flying condition….)

Air time was 0900 to 1455 hours—in that six hours a whole lifetime passed before us….

—PERSONAL DIARY

GROUND CREW AND ORDNANCE

B-25 MITCHELL

We were hit by twin-engine German fighters. They sprayed the formation with 20mm cannon and were out of range of our 50-cal. guns most of the time. Lewis had about 80% of tail turret blown up around him. Part of the shell ripped out his oxygen regulator right next to his left shoulder and also cut the electrical wiring to the turret. There was a cloud of blue-grey smoke in the tail and for this reason, we believe it was an explosive shell. We also heard a loud report. Lewis did not answer calls on the inter-com and I proceeded back to the tail turret. To this day, I do not know if he was aware of the fact that I was in back of him, but he fell into my arms just as I reached him. He was pulled out of the turret in a dazed condition and complained of his shoulder hurting. It was too cold to remove his clothing, so I put my hand inside his outer-garments to his underwear. When I withdrew my hand, there was no blood on it, and Lewis was sent to the flight deck to regain his composure. I got into the tail turret and found that the guns would not fire; however, it was possible to move the turret manually, so I stayed there because moving guns would indicate to the fighters that the position was still manned. Someone of the crew kept me supplied with refilled walk-around oxygen bottles.

—PERSONAL DIARY, 12 APRIL 1944

NOSE-GUNNER, B-24 LIBERATOR

B-17 FLYING FORTRESSES

APRIL 29, 1944. Went to Toulon, France, where the target was a munitions plant. Boy, what a lot of flak...red, white, black puffs all around us. We only got one little hole in the ship. We had no fighters attack us, though we saw a few fighters attack another bomb group. They put up enough flak for us to walk on, but it was short of our altitude. The red bursts appeared as we were leaving the target. We think that this was the anti-aircraft gunners way of telling the fighters that they were ceasing fire, and that it was up to them to pursue us if they were going to. This also told their fighter pilots that they could dive through our formations without the fear of being hit by their own flak.

—PERSONAL DIARY

BALL TURRET, B-17 FLYING FORTRESS

MAY 18, 1944. Ploesti, Romania. All of us ran short of gas..."Coming in on a wing and a prayer" really means something after one of these runs. We saw several P-38's ditch their planes because they were out of gas and our bombers flew circles around them and dropped life rafts to them—in the Adriatic—and radioed their position to the Air-Sea Rescue. Eleven planes had to land at Bari, Italy, because of gas shortage. We shot flares at our home base to be given priority to land, because we knew our gas supply was all but gone. As we taxied to our revetment one engine stopped—dry well, and as we turned around to park on the revetment, another engine quit on us.

—PERSONAL DIARY

B-24 LIBERATOR

They have a public address system throughout the barracks and they play a recording of reveille. This is immediately followed by a full-volume blast of Benny Goodman's "Idaho." If we are not out of bed by then, they follow with some Harlem maniacs' recording of "Cow Boogie."

—PERSONAL ACCOUNT

GENTLEMEN, A TOAST

When I return from Italy with mud upon my feet,

With mud upon my pants and shirt, mud in every pleat,

With mud beneath my fingernails, mud all through my hair,

I'll step into the nearest bar and climb upon a chair;

Then I'll announce to all the world: I've mud inside me, too,

And since I have to wash it out, the drinks are all on you;

But let me warn you 'fore you start, I'll shoot the first damn guy

Who raises up his glass and toasts, "Well, here's mud in your eye."

CHUNGKING, CHINA, 13 June 1942. (Chennault) was completely responsible for development of the tactics which enabled the Flying Tigers, using slower and inferior P-40s, to outperform the best Jap Zeros. Chennault devised the "hit and run" tactics and thoroughly imbued his pilots against the idea of engaging in prolonged dog-fights with the Japs. The Japs feared him as much as any man in the Far East and put a price on his head, dead or alive. Deaf as a post, Chennault would sit around in conferences like a cigar-store Indian. However, he was a good lip-reader and his agile mind followed everything closely.... Although he had a reputation for being damned tough, he had a fatherly way with his men. They all loved him.

—GENERAL LEWIS H. BRERETON

P-40 WARHAWK

B-17 FLYING FORTRESS

MAY 14, 1944. We took off at 0920, the target was Piacenza Airdrome at San Desenzano, Italy. We had 240 fragmentary bombs aboard. We encountered no flak nor fighters at the target, but came within from two to five feet of getting much worse. Our own B-17's were 2,000 feet overhead—right over our formation and were dropping their payload One of the bombs passed right between our engines #3 and #4...another barely missed the waist gun by 2 feet. Boy, all of us were really praying.

—PERSONAL DIARY

C-46 COMMANDO

We were pretty bewildered most of the time because we wanted to fly, and we got madder and madder the more the Japs raided Clark Field (Philippines), which was often. After the first attack, living conditions were pretty bad. We lived in nipa shacks (made out of reeds) or in rifle butts. We didn't have any tents. These places were something like dugouts, and we did all our cooking, sleeping, and everything there. No one ever took a bath. I don't think any of us changed clothes during the first week. Everything was filthy. Everything was covered with dust, and the filth hurt our morale worse than the Japs did.

—LIEUTENANT PETE BENDER, DECEMBER 1941

The Greyhound Bus System not only turned their transportation capabilities into a war effort, they made a technicolor film entitled, "This Amazing America," to help satisfy soldiers homesick for another glimpse of their homeland. The film is a pictorial journey across America. It was shown at outposts, in hospitals, on transports, and before battles to boost morale.

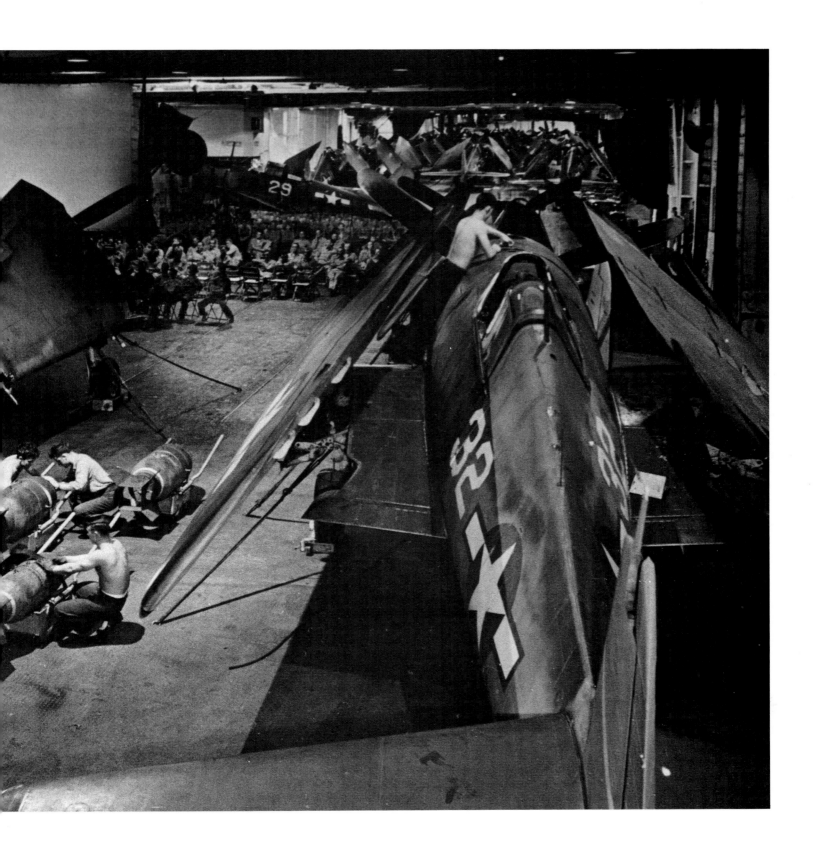

When the Teatro Mercantile was not presenting operas or stage shows, GI's would fill its hard wooden seats to watch the latest cinema antics of Bing Crosby, Betty Hutton, Abbott and Costello, or Bette Davis. Directed by the Red Cross and the Army Special Services, most of the more recent movie productions were shown on the screen of the Italian theatre with, of course, a five minute wait every half hour while the operator changed reels. These movies, however, were an escape from the country that we were in, an escape from the life that we were living. Once again we could see America, an automobile, a nightclub, a well-dressed woman. Our over-taxed memories could relax, and we would be walking once more on the sidewalks of Broadway, Main Street, Water Street, Fifth Avenue, or Sunset Boulevard.

—PERSONAL ACCOUNT

B-29 SUPERFORTRESS

B-29 SUPERFORTRESS

Take advantage of opportunities afforded you when the air-raid sirens sound
the warning of attack or blackout. For example:

    A. If in a bakery, grab a pie.

    B. If in a tavern, grab a beer.

    C. If in a theater, grab a blonde.

—a wag's response to air-raid instructions in Hawaii after the bombing of Pearl Harbor,

December 1941

INVASION FORCE

The tempo of a successful war is progressive. We have to do all we can and then immediately double it. The enemy can stand the kind of blows that we gave him last year even though they were heavy and though they hurt him. What he cannot stand and what we can and must give him are those redoubled blows.

—SPEECH BY GENERAL HENRY H. ARNOLD, 30 DECEMBER 1943

P-47 THUNDERBOLT

P-40 WARHAWK

We have learned how to win a war in
this air age. Our best hope for a long
and secure peace lies in remembering
what we have learned.
—Robert A. Lovett, Assistant Secretary of
War for Air, September 1944

CLASSICS would have been impossible without the help of many friends, businesses, and supporters. To find, fly, and photograph the aircraft you see on these pages took three years of planning and a year and a half of shooting. These color pictures were selected from over 10,000 35mm slides, and present a cross section of the finest restored World War II aircraft in the world. Each of these airplanes is a flying work of art, representing thousands of hours of effort and major amounts of money to restore, fly, and maintain. In a sense, this book is a museum catalog of some of America's finest flying warbirds.

Air-to-air photography is difficult without superb pilots, planning, and precise execution. Robbie Robinson, Dale Krebsbach, and Jack Moore flew the B-25 camera plane for most of the air-to-air photography in CLASSICS. Bill Arnot, Mike Pupich, Craig Timms, and R.L. Waltrip also loaned their B-25s as camera planes when Robbie's B-25, "Chapter XI," was not available. These marvelous airplanes provided a first-class seat facing aft for me to take pictures. I was privileged to work with some of the best warbird pilots flying today. Gentlemen like Howard Pardue, Rudy Frasca, Hess Bomberger, Pete McManus, Archie Donahue, and J.K. West flew formation on my camera ship, sometimes so close that I could read their lips as we talked on the radio. I would have been unable to make these pictures without the skills of these and many other pilots and aircrews who flew for my cameras. Thanks again to all of you.

I must also thank Arnold Drapkin and the editors at TIME magazine for giving me the time and encouragement to tackle the huge project that CLASSICS became. To the photojournalist, time and access are priceless commodities: TIME helped with both. Kodachrome film and Leica cameras faithfully captured the scenes that unfolded, flight after flight. Most of the shooting for CLASSICS was done with Leica R4 cameras, and 35mm, 90mm, and 180mm lenses. The new 35mm 1.4 Summilux became a kind of time machine for me during the hectic days of shooting. With its added ability to gather light, I was able to shoot one-half hour earlier and one-half hour later each day. This bonus of extra time allowed me to capture a very special kind of light and mood which can be seen throughout CLASSICS.

As always, safety was our first concern during the shooting of this book. My friend and assistant, Ted Reynolds, and I wore safety gear from Adventure Specialists in Miami, Florida, for each flight. Many times I was looking out through nothing but air and sunshine to the plane I was photographing. With a dependable safety harness on, I had one less thing to worry about. Ken Hansen and his staff came to my rescue during the shooting of CLASSICS. Being able to replace a broken camera or lens overnight from Ken's stock of Leica equipment was invaluable.

Unintentionally, I'm sure I've left out people who helped make CLASSICS a reality. To each of you who helped change this dream into a book we can hold in our hands, thank you!

—MARK MEYER

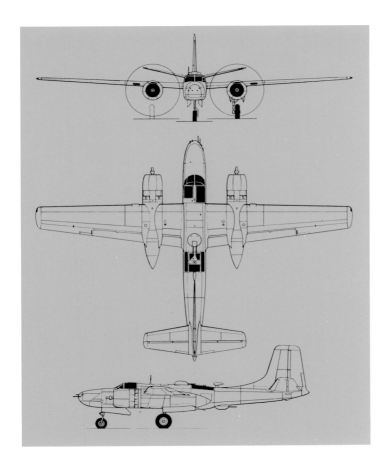

A-26 INVADER

The powerful, quick, and heavily armed A-26 Invader was designed in 1940, and the first prototype flew in July 1942. This aircraft—the culmination of the development of the A-20 series—was one of the best ground-attack and tactical bombers used by the United States.

Heavy machine guns were mounted in the nose section, and four additional heavy machine guns were installed in remote-control turrets. The power of this aircraft lay in its ability to add another ten externally mounted machine guns on certain missions. When this extra strength was coupled with the Invader's formidable bomb-load, the aircraft possessed lethal power.

The A-26C, the last of the three Invader variants, was completed in 1945. It was a more conventionally designed aircraft, having a glazed nose and less armament.

After the end of the war, the A-26 Invader remained in service, and these aircraft played an active part in both the Korean and Vietnam wars.

Manufacturer: Douglas Aircraft Company **Type:** bomber, ground-attack **Engine:** two Pratt & Whitney R-2800-27 Double Wasp 18-cylinder radial air-cooled, 2,000 hp each **Dimensions:** wingspan 70 feet, length 50 feet 9 inches, height 18 feet 6 inches **Weight:** 35,000 pounds (loaded) **Speed:** 355 mph maximum, 280 mph cruise **Ceiling:** 31,300 feet **Range:** 1,800 miles **Armament:** 10 machine guns, 4,000 pounds of bombs **Crew:** 3

Photographs: p. 102

209

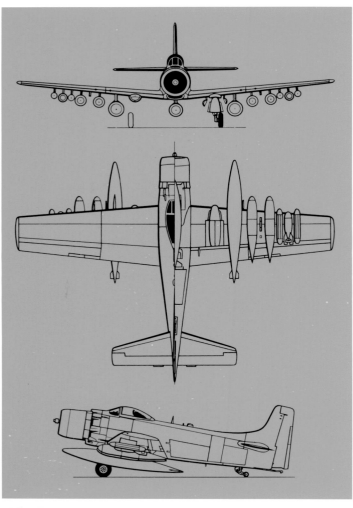

AD-1 SKYRAIDER

Between 1945 and 1957 seven versions of the Skyraider were produced. The first prototype, the XBT2D-1, flew in March 1945, less than one year after the project began. By December 1946, the first AD-1 models flew into combat. The great potential of its airframe led to the development of new variants, which were the last of the heavy, single-seat, piston-engine, combat aircraft developed.

From the beginning, the AD Skyraider series showed great potential, and each model incorporated additional enhancements. One common feature shared by earlier variants was their ability to fly as day-assault, all-weather assault, radar surveillance, or electronic countermeasures air-craft.

The AD-5, designed in 1951, was a sophisticated aircraft with enough space for two crewmen to sit side-by-side in a wide cockpit. This innovative design was discarded in 1952, however, with the production of the single-seat assault configuration of the AD-6 and the powerful AD-7, produced in 1955.

The versatility of the AD Skyraider family kept the aircraft in action through the late 1970s as a ground-attack plane.

Manufacturer: Douglas Aircraft Company   **Type:** reconnaissance, ground-attack   **Engine:** Wright R-3350-26W Cyclone 18-cylinder radial air-cooled, 2,700 hp   **Dimensions:** wingspan 50 feet; length AD-5W—40 feet 1 inch, AD-6—39 feet 2 inches; height AD-5W—15 feet 10 inches, AD-6—15 feet 8 inches   **Weight:** 25,500 pounds (loaded)   **Speed:** AD-5W—311 mph maximum at 18,000 feet; AD-6—322 mph maximum at 18,000 feet   **Ceiling:** AD-5W—27,000 feet; AD-6—28,500 feet   **Range:** AD-5W—1,294 miles; AD-6—1,143 miles   **Armament:** AD-5W—2 × 20mm cannon; AD-6—4 × 20mm cannon, 8,000 pounds of bombs   **Crew:** AD-5W—3; AD-6—1

Photographs: pp. 90-91, p. 92, p.93

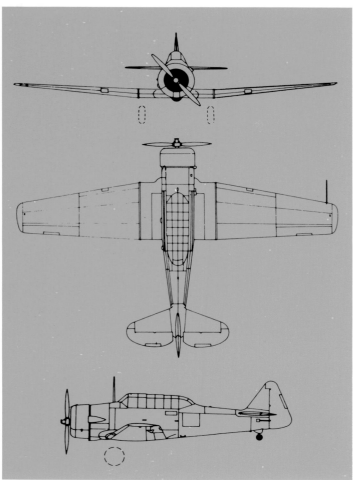

AT-6 TEXAN

The first production models of the AT-6 Texan appeared in the U.S. in 1940 and were the "twin" of the Australian Wirraway, manufactured by Commonwealth Aircraft. Although the new aircraft incorporated many of the latest technological advancements, the AT-6 maintained the same general lines and structure of its predecessor, North American's BT-9 trainer. (Earlier the BT-9 had been improved to create the NA-33, which the Australians had adopted for their Wirraway line.) The main difference between the AT-6 and the BT-9 was the Texan's new, retractable landing-gear.

Five variants of the AT-6 were produced, and small modifications were made to each new model. The AT-6A utilized a different engine and fuel tanks; the AT-6B was intended for use in airgunner training; the AT-6C introduced specific structural modifications to save aluminum; the AT-6D returned to the original design. The final design, the AT-6F, was also the most powerful.

AT-6 Texan monoplanes proved to be so safe and durable that today the planes are still used by many military air forces.

Manufacturer: North American Aviation, Inc.   **Type:** trainer   **Engine:** AT-6A—Pratt & Whitney R-1340-49 Wasp 9-cylinder radial air-cooled, 600 hp   **Dimensions:** wingspan 42 feet, length 29 feet, height 11 feet 9 inches   **Weight:** 5,300 pounds (loaded)   **Speed:** 208 mph maximum   **Ceiling:** 24,200 feet   **Range:** 750 miles   **Armament:** 2 machine guns   **Crew:** 2

Photographs: pp. 48-49; NA-33, p. 52; p. 53

The photographer gratefully acknowledges the assistance of the following individuals, whose gracious cooperation made this book possible: John Abramo, Vick Agather, John Alger, Ben Anderson, Neil Anderson, Bill Arnot, Bud Arnot, Tom Austin, Dick Baird, George Baker, Lynne Barber, John T. Baugh, Dick Baughman, Dellon Baumgardner, Nelda Baumgardner, James Beasley, Bill Becker, John Bell II, Ralph Benhart, Bob Blankenship, Ruthie Blankenship, Dick Bodycombe, Hess Bomberger, Connie Bowlin, Ed Bowlin, Bob Byrne, Chris Campbell, Vince Carruth, Bill Carter, Jane Carter, Dick Caum, Mary Alice Caum, George Clark, William E. Clark, Glenn Coleman, Joe Coleman, Mike Collier, Bob Collings, Mike Collins, Buddy Cooksey, Bill Crump, Jay Cullum, Dean Cutshaw, Bill Dahlgren, Dick Daum, Don Davidson, Dick Deiter, Tom Deiter, John Dilley, Dennis Divine, Bill Dodds, Archie Donahue, Lyn Dowling, Pat Elliot, Bob Ellis, John Ellis, Joe Engle, Dick Ervin, Joan Ervin, Jeff Ethell, Susan Ewing, Dude Ezel, Nelson Ezel, Debbie Fetherston, Jennifer Fierro, Joe Frasca, Rudy Frasca, Lynn Gamma, Marvin L. Gardner, Ronnie Gardner, Bob Gear, Bill Godwin, John Goltra, Bill Greenwood, Wanda Gurr, Nelson Hall, Francis Hancock, H.M. Hancock, Roy Harris, Bill Harrison, John Hess, Tex Hill, Jack Hilliard, John Hinton, Steve Hinton, Jack Holden, Bill Holm, Christa Holm, Eddie Holmes, Jimmie Hunt, Charles Hutchins, David Karlson, John Kelley, Fred Kirk, Jim Kitchens, Bill Klaers, Dale Krebsbach, Sally Kyle, Kermit LaQuey, Kevin Larosa, Brenda Lofton, Harold Longberry, Howard Loveling, Jim Lowe, Joe Mabee, Ray Mabrey, Glen MacDonald, Leland L. Martin, Dan McCue, Danny McGee, Carter McGreggor, Jimmy McMillion, Pete McManus, Joe McShane III, Harry Merritt, Bob Mikesh, Madge Minton, Art Monig, Jack Moore, Julie Moore, Lloyd Nolen, Bill Northcut, Howard Pardue, Georgia Parrish, Pete Parrish, Sue Parrish, Oz Parrish, Ernie Persich, Walt Pine, Paul Poberezny, Tom Poppell, Sam Poss, Ed Pupek, Mike Pupich, Tom Reilly, Carol Reynolds, Ted Reynolds, Buck Ridley, Chris Robinson, Gary Robinson, Peaches Robinson, Rick Ropke, Bill Ross, Ralph Royce, Scott Royce, Bill Russell, Jack Sadler, Rob Satterfield, Jaime Serra, Ari Silberman, John Silberman, Jack Skipper, Guy Joe Smith, John Souther, Bob Spaulding, Moon Spillers, George St George, Charles Stolenberg, Ann Strine, Russ Strine, Cory Stutzman, Ray Stutzman, Ray Thompson, Craig Timms, Walt Trainer, Joe Underwood, Richard Upstrom, R.L. Waltrip, Jack Webster, Pat Webster, Kermitt Weeks, J.K. West, Jean Winkler, Arthur Wolk, Tom Wood, Walter Wooten, Jim Zazas, Tony Ziemiecki.

The publisher gratefully acknowledges the kind cooperation of Henry R. Beeson, Joseph S. Bochna, A. Hess Bomberger, Matt Carmack, Philip O. Carr, Archie Donahue, and David Lee "Tex" Hill.

With special thanks to F. Bradley Peyton III, for sharing his memories and personal materials, among them the diaries of Warren Hearn, Kirby H. Woehst, George M. Foote, and Herbert W. Gray, all members of the crew of "Tailwind," a B-24 Liberator of the 738th Squadron, 454th Bombardment Group (Heavy), 15th Army Air Force. Special thanks also to the press staff of Vice President George H. Bush for their assistance with his interview.